1 MONTH OF
FREE
READING

at
www.ForgottenBooks.com

---◇---

By purchasing this book you are
eligible for one month membership to
ForgottenBooks.com, giving you
unlimited access to our entire
collection of over 1,000,000 titles via
our web site and mobile apps.

To claim your free month visit:
www.forgottenbooks.com/free742743

ISBN 978-0-483-41509-6
PIBN 10742743

This book is a reproduction of an important historical work. Forgotten Books uses
state-of-the-art technology to digitally reconstruct the work, preserving the original format
whilst repairing imperfections present in the aged copy. In rare cases, an imperfection in
the original, such as a blemish or missing page, may be replicated in our edition. We do,
however, repair the vast majority of imperfections successfully; any imperfections that
remain are intentionally left to preserve the state of such historical works.

HOLINESS TO THE LORD

THE JUVENILE

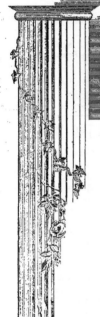

. **Vol. XXXII.**   **APRIL 15, 1897.**   **No. 8.**

CONTENTS.

PROFESSIONALS.

THE JUVENILE INSTRUCTOR.

Organ for Young Latter Day Saints

Vol. XXXII.   SALT LAKE CITY, APRIL 15, 1897.   No. 8.

THE PIONEERS AND OTHERS.

What They Did and How They Did It.

II.—THE MARCH OF EMPIRE.

THE ground having been broken the work of beating back the silent but stubborn forces of solitude and wildness in the Far West went grandly on. The nucleus was established when the first wagon emerged from the rugged jaws of Emigration Canyon, and thereafter the forces of civilization gathered and grew and became more and more a power and a joy as time wore along. The first structure of any kind that was reared in Salt Lake valley was naturally enough a place for public meetings. The groves were God's first temples, and this particular outpost of His cause was not greatly different, being a bowery. It was erected near the spot where Assembly Hall now stands and was as crude and primitive an affair as could be and afford any shelter at all. As a matter of fact it did not protect the inmates from rain or high winds and they never expected it would; as a means of warding off the rays of the sun, however, it was a conspicuous success. It was begun two days after the arrival here, and its construction, being free from the entanglements of high-priced architects and contractors and its constituent elements existing in rank profusion on every hand, did not require a great deal of time. The next season a larger and more pretentious bowery was built, in which a stage was subsequently constructed, and here for the first time in the shadows of the Rocky Mountains and still hedged around and about with primeval desolation, the first dramatic entertainment was given. The play was "Robert Macaire;" Philip Margetts, who is still on this stage of action and almost as lively as ever, enacted the comedy part and established himself at once as a prime favorite. He has not forgotten how the "old thing worked," and has advanced with the advancement of the times, but he only occasionally of late years affords us a taste of his quality. The first building for dramatic representations was the Social Hall in this city; it still stands where it was erected, but during the past score of years has not been used for theatrical purposes. It is now the home of a Physical Culture Class, and has at times degenerated even into being the scene of political meetings. The last People's party convention of Salt Lake County was held in it four years ago, and the writer was chairman. The chair was mounted on a platform which was a trifle too narrow for both a table and chair, and while "holding down" a heated debate and pounding the table into splinters with an improvised gavel (a walking stick) the chair was inadvertently edged a little too far back, and went over, taking its occupant along with it and bringing the debate to a sudden and unlooked-for termination. It also brought something else in the shape of anger-provoking merriment, but this need not be dwelt upon.

The first crop in Utah was no crop at all, if such a milesianism can be permitted. None of the patatoes was larger than a good-sized marble, and they were useful only for seed next year. This calls to mind the oft-quoted remark of "old Jim Bridger;" when hearing where the Pioneers had decided to make their homes, he said he would give a thousand dollars for the first ear of corn raised on this soil. It looked for a while as if he had taken about the right view of it, but the people had, like many of the country newspapers, "come to stay," and unlike the great majority of such publications, succeeded in doing it. Looking beyond their discouragement and casting their disappointment to the winds, they plodded along as earnestly and persistently as though fortune was smiling as broadly as the man in the moon when it (the moon) is full. Residences of logs and adobe became quite numerous, and were steadily improved and added to. Fences were the next adjunct of civilization in evidence, and had there been enough to eat the people would scarcely have realized that they were having any trouble at all.

The power of the press was neither forgotten nor overlooked. Two years after the arrival here a printing outfit, as complete as the means and facilities at hand would admit of, was obtained in the East and brought to this city, where in due season the *Deseret News* made its appearance as a weekly publication. It was a small affair, but large enough for the time and place and was a long way ahead of many we have had since. It proved to be an impetus in the direction of fostering and forwarding modern influences whose importance was scarcely realized at the time. The press on which it was printed was a "Ramage," worked with a crank and lever, the bed being about 18 by 24

JIM BRIDGER.

inches and in the hands of an able-bodied expert could be made to turn out as many as 200 impressions an hour. Many years after this beginning the writer became an apprentice in the *News* office, and worked that same press till he was tired enough to behave himself when not so engaged. It is still in the possession of the *News* establishment, and while for years past an utterly useless appendage, it would not be disposed of for many times its original cost, which was some $200 laid down here. This goes to show that times have changed and we have done a little in that line as well.

The next paper to be established in Utah was the *Mountaineer*, which was "flung to the breeze" in 1859. It was a pretty good publication for those times; James Ferguson, a man of capacity and culture, was editor, and the civil war. I have a recollection of the state of excitement into which the community was thrown when the news of the great battle of Bull Run reached us; it was on everybody's lips and for a time business was fairly suspended. But Brother Ferguson's paper published the details—four or five columns of them—bristling with intensely lurid, graphic and exciting paragraphs without a sub-heading, cross line or other dis-

PRESIDENT TAYLOR'S FIRST RESIDENCE, OLD FORT BLOCK, 1847.

he had "a happy faculty of "stirring up the animals" now and then which was enjoyed even by those who preferred the more staid and quiet methods of the *News* as a steady diet. A perusal of some of the files of the *Mountaineer* and contrasting them with the papers of to-day is a very entertaining performance. Like its neighbor it eschewed big head-lines, even when the pony express brought in the most startling news of tinguishing feature except the one line at the top in pica bold face, "Latest News!" (The exclamation point is mine; the paper referred to would not go so far as that in the direction of engendering heart disease among its readers.) It died in the second year of the war, the constant strain upon its conservative tendencies by reason of the prevailing and increasing agitation in the East and excitement at home proving too much for it at last. Its editor soon followed, his demise being the occasion of sincere and general sorrow.

Previous to this another printing equipment had found its way to Utah, but was not put to use at once. It was the property of the late Joseph E. Johnson, a veteran journalist, an indefatigable worker and an uncompromising Democrat. When the company in which the writer set sail for Utah arrived at Wood River, Nebraska, there were two houses there, one occupied by Mr. Johnson, the other by some one else; and there, a hundred miles or so from anywhere, with no neighbors to speak of, no traffic but what the passing emigrant trains created, he lived, thrived and—started a paper! It was called the *Huntsman's Echo*, and was discontinued immediately after our train passed. Whether one event was the cause of the other, or whether the two were merely coincidents, I have not yet learned. He brought the outfit to Utah with him and two or three papers were subsequently published with it. The press is now in the possession of his son Charles E., the well known photographer of this city.

A paper called the *Valley Tan* was established here about 1859 and "hung on by its eyebrows" for about a year; while it passed away before the writer's advent, he saw several copies of it. It seemed to have had a serious case of rabies, which had struck in and become incurable. It never stooped to argument, and rarely got down so low as to resort to the plainer and more commonplace facts. The mention of the word "Mormon" seems to have been enough to throw the editor into spasms; his name was Kirk Anderson, and he had the reputation of being the homeliest man in Utah. (This is not mentioned as a cause of reproach by any means; a great many people would seriously object to being gauged by such a standard, and the writer is one of them). A man may be very good and yet not good looking; but Mr. Anderson was, according to the evidence, somewhat otherwise. He was a Mormon hater of such pronounced proclivities that they must at times have affected his appetite. His paper soon filled an unhonored grave while he drifted away and has forgotten to return. No one, so far as I could learn, ever went to look for him.

It is one of the singular things of our journalistic history that the first daily paper in Utah was published at Fort Douglas. This was in 1861, the editor being Charles H. Hempstead, then an officer at the post, but subsequently a lawyer of this city. He has been dead several years.

S. A. Kenner.

(TO BE CONTINUED.)

ROBINSON CRUSOE'S ISLAND.

YOUNG America and young England and, indeed, all Young Christendom have suffered a grievous loss, says a writer in the *New York Herald*, in speaking of the swallowing up of Robinson Crusoe's island.

But was Juan Fernandez the island of Robinson Crusoe? Yes, and no, but mainly yes. Robinson Crusoe, you may remember, was wrecked on the east coast of South America. Now, if you take down your atlas you will find that Juan Fernandez lies on the west coast of South America, some three hundred miles out from Chili. But what matters such minor detail? De Foe's narrative was part truth and part fiction but it was founded on the truthful story of Alexander Selkirk, who lived on this island in absolute isolation for over four years, and was finally rescued in 1709.

A word, then, about the history of Juan Fernandez. It received its name from its discoverer, a Spanish navigator, who first landed there in 1563, and later revisited it to found a settlement, taking with him a few families and a number of goats. This is probably the origin of these animals in the island, as no mention is made of their having existed there before. Eventually this colony was broken up by the superior inducements held out to settlers in Chili, which at that time fell under the dominion of the Spaniards.

Still another anticipatory Crusoe was a certain Musquito Indian, who was accidentally left behind by the English captain, Watlin, in 1681 and was rescued three years later by Captain Dampier. This Indian, Dampier tells us, "had with him his gun and a knife, with a small horn of powder and a few shot, which, being spent, he contrived a way by notching his knife to saw the barrel of his gun into small pieces, wherewith he made harpoons, lances, hooks and a long knife, heating the pieces first in the fire, which he struck with his gun flint, and a piece of the barrel of his gun, which he hardened, having learned to do that among the English." With such rude instruments as he made in that manner, he procured an abundant supply of provisions, chiefly goats and fish. Dampier put out a canoe from the vessel, and went ashore to look for the Musquito man.

When they saw him "he had no clothes left, having worn out those he brought from Watlin's ship, but only a skin about his waist." The scene that ensued is quaintly and touchingly described in the simple language of the narrative. "He saw our ship the day before we came to an anchor," says Dampier, "and believed we were English, and therefore killed two goats in the morning before we came to an anchor and dressed them with cabbage, to treat us when we came ashore. He came then to the seaside to congratulate our safe arrival. And when we landed a Musquito Indian named Robin first leapt ashore, and, running to his brother Musquito man, threw himself flat on his face, who, helping him up and embracing him, and when their ceremonies of civility were over we also that stood gazing at them drew near, each of us embracing him we had found here, who was overjoyed to see so many of his old friends, come hither, as he thought, purposely to fetch him."

And now at last we come to the story of Alexander Selkirk. In February, 1709, Captain Woodes Rodgers, commander of two privateers belonging to Bristol, arrived in the neighborhood of the island. According to the Capain's own narrative it appears that when the ships came near the land a light was discovered, which it was thought must be on board a ship at anchor. Two French vessels had been cruising in search of Captain Rodgers' vessel, and these vessels they supposed to be lying in wait for them close to the shore. The boats which had started for the shore returned, and preparations were made for action. On the following day, seeing no vessel there, they went ashore, where they found a man clothed in goat skins, looking, as the narrator says, "wilder than the first owners of them." His name was Alexander Selkirk, a Scotchman, who had been master of the Cinque Ports. Having quarreled with

Captain Stradling, under whose command he sailed, he was left ashore at his own request, preferring solitude on an unknown island to the life he led on board this vessel. Before the boat that put him ashore left the beach he repented of his resolution, and begged to be taken back again; but his companions cruelly mocked him and left him to his fate. It was he that made the fire which had attracted the attention of the two privateers. They took him on board, and, being a good officer, well recommended by Captain Dampier, he was appointed mate on board Captain Rodgers' vessel and taken to England.

Robinson Crusoe, in any event, cannot be considered altogether a work of fiction. Without adhering strictly to the actual adventures of Selkirk or of the castaways who preceded him, it gives, in the descriptions of scenery, the mode of providing food, the rude experiments resorted to for shelter against the weather, and all the trials and consolations of solitude, a faithfully drawn picture from these narratives, and a most truthful and charming delineation of solitary life, with such reflections as the subject naturally suggested. De Foe was the great medium through which the spirit of the whole was fused; it required the splendor of his genius to preserve from oblivion the lessons therein taught—of the advantages of temperance, fortitude, and above all, an implicit reliance in the wisdom and mercy of the Creator. He represents them in a most fascinating garb, with all the originality of master mind; and it detracts nothing from his credit to say that the pictures are drawn strictly from nature.

Crusoe's Cave, for such is the name which Selkirk's former abode persistently maintains, is one hundred yards inland from a little cove in what is known as Crusoe's Valley. It lies in a volcanic mass of rock, forming the bluff or termination of a rugged rock, and looks as if it might be the doorway into the ruins of some grand old castle. The interior is less imposing. It is an ordinary cavern, about twelve feet high, fifteen feet deep and twenty feet wide at the entrance, and resembles in shape an old fashioned brick oven. It is now occupied only by wild goats and bats.

We have only had staccato information of the condition and number of the inhabitants. Every now and then a ship touches at Juan Fernandez, and some passenger makes a record of what he has seen and heard. In 1849 J. Ross Browne found sixteen persons on the island, consisting of William Pearce, an American, and four or five Chilian men with their wives and children. An anonymous writer in Putnam's Magazine for 1868 reckons the total number at about a dozen, among them probably the same William Pearce, for he describes him as a white North American who was said to have been the mate of a whaler and to have purposely suffered himself to be left behind by his ship some years before our arrival. The man had formed a marriage with a Chilian woman on the island by whom he subsequently had several children. He expressed the intention of passing the remainder of his life in the place, and seemed quite happy and contented with that prospect.

"The houses, or rather huts," says this authority, "in which these people lived, were so exactly like Robinson Crusoe's as described by De Foe, in materials structure and appearance, as to be, for those familiar with the story, exceedingly striking. The inhabitants, too, wore goat skins, and their primitive and shaggy appearance was equally suggestive of the famous romance. They knew all about the latter, and about Selkirk, their predecessor on the island, and showed a cave, the remains of a log hut, and various other things which they alleged the Scotch sailor had built, lived in or made."

The island in area is about fifteen miles long by five or six wide.

TOPICS OF THE TIMES.

OUR LATE GENERAL CONFERENCE.

THE observation is frequently made after a conference has been held, whether a quarterly conference in the Stakes or a general conference, that it was the "best conference we ever had."

While this may not always be the case, still it is a good sign for the people to feel that the conference has been one of the best, because it shows that they have been benefited by the teachings and have appreciated the spirit which prevailed. It would not, perhaps, be altogether true to say that our late general conference in Salt Lake City was the best one which we have had, but it is true to say that it was an excellent one, and that both speakers and hearers enjoyed to a goodly degree the outpourings of the spirit of the Lord. Instructions were given which will prove very valuable to the Saints if they will be carried out. Recent events among us have called attention to the Priesthood and its powers and authority. These have been more clearly defined than usual. The necessity for doing so has been very apparent of late, and while the instructions that have been given may need to be repeated often before they will correct the mistaken views that some have been led to

entertain, still great good will undoubtedly result from that which has already been said. Where people have yielded to wrong influences, or imbibed a spirit of darkness, or indulged in misconceptions concerning the authority of the Priesthood, it takes time to correct them.

Even with time it would be impossible for any man to induce a people as numerous as the Latter-day Saints to view doctrines and policy from one standpoint if the Lord did not aid them. His spirit, and His spirit alone, can make Latter-day Saints perceive and understand the truth and keep them united. To bring about entire union, therefore, His power must be invoked and His assistance, through the Holy Ghost, must be obtained. It is upon the Lord's spirit that the Elders must depend. It constitutes the power by which correct doctrine can be enforced upon the people, and to its heavenly influence the present union of the Latter-day Saints can be attributed.

The only drawback to the conference was the absence of President Woodruff through sickness, but all were delighted to see him on the last day, his health then permitting him to take part in the conference.

One of the grievous features of the times is the number of unemployed people in our communities. It is a painful sight to see men and women willing to work without the opportunity of working. This is especially so where people come from other lands in obedience to the Gospel. They reach Zion willing to unite themselves with the people here but find themselves destitute of employment. Some of those who come from afar to this land have been accustomed all their lives to working for wages, and are as helpless as children in furnishing themselves with work. They have never had their faculties exercised in providing for themselves and in managing and planning so as to provide themselves with labor. Western people, who have had experience such as the Latter-day Saints have gone through, are very seldom at a loss for something to do. Their minds have been brightened by experience and the necessities of the situations in which they have been placed. The people who first came to these valleys found plenty of employment. They had very little to begin with. They had no knowledge of the climate, or of the soil, or of irrigation, but their previous experience prepared them to grapple with the difficulties which surrounded them. They built houses, cultivated the soil and watered their crops. They raised their food, and they prospered. But those who come in now, many of them not having had experience, look around them in a helpless fashion, and unless somebody furnishes them with employment they know not what to do. If they were not helped they would starve in the midst of the plenty which abounds on every hand.

To people of experience, such as the pioneers had, there is no need for anyone to go idle. Good openings for making a living are to be seen on every hand, yet persons without experience rarely see them. But these people who do not have this knowledge have come here in obedience to the command of the Lord. They want to live in Zion, they want to help build up Zion, but they do not know how. Must they be left to starve or to go back to where they came from, dissatisfied and disappointed? Certainly not. It is the duty of the Latter-day Saints to do something

to help these people, to teach them how to make a living. The Elders who have gone out to preach the Gospel have spent years of time in converting the Saints who come here; but when they are converted that does not end the work of salvation, either temporal or spiritual. Others must then take hold and contribute to the work of saving them by teaching them how to apply their labor in a proper manner to earn a living.

This is one of the topics that was brought to the attention of the Priesthood meeting during the conference, and to the meeting of the leading officers of the Church on the day succeeding the conference. It is to be hoped that steps will be taken looking to the providing of labor for the unemployed and for the care of the Saints who gather from afar to these valleys, that they should not be left to wander around without direction and guidance. It is not possible to furnish every one who comes here with the employment to which he or she has been accustomed in the land from whence they have been gathered. But it is perhaps possible to furnish them with some employment that will contribute, if not entirely, at least in some degree, toward their sustenence, and enable them to obtain the training that will be of value to them hereafter. If any successful plans shall be adopted towards these ends through the meetings of the late general conference, then the Latter-day Saints will have cause to congratulate themselves on that much being accomplished.

The Editor.

THE gloomy and the resentful are usually found among those who have nothing to do or who do nothing.

TAHITI AND THE SOCIETY ISLAND MISSION.

(CONTINUED FROM PAGE 226.)

At the expiration of the sentence of the brethren who were taken to Tahiti and compelled to work for two years at hard labor, those that did not apostatize returned to Anaa and continued their worship. Bible classes and meetings where he was stopping, with an escort of ten soldiers, and arrested eight of the leading brethren and two of the sisters.

After the brethren being kept in jail for about a week, and the sisters being watched over in the Government building, they dressed themselves in their best clothes and with Bibles under their arms were ushered into the presence of

CELEBRATION OF FOURTEENTH OF JULY.

were conducted as usual. It was some little time after 1862 that the Saints living at the village of Otepipi were complained of by outside natives to the Resident Governor that they were rebelling against the French Government. Accordingly the Governor came across the lagoon from the village of Tunhora the Governor, by the escort of soldiers, five being guard in front and five in the rear. After some questioning being done, the two sisters and three of the brethren were set at liberty, but the five, who were the most prominent, were taken to Tuuhora. Their names were Pake, Tuaanapohe, Temahu, Tihoni, and Maihea. The first three named gained their liberty by promising not to pray or preach any more, but their Bibles were taken from them by the Governor. Tiboni and Maihea would not promise so they were sent to spend the night in jail. By morning a change of heart had come over the Governor, who had the two brethren brought before him and set them at liberty with permission to return to their homes and pray and preach as much as they liked.

Thus they continued without being hindered much, until after the year 1879. In this year the different islands were swept over by a tidal wave which destroyed many of the houses and most of the cocoanut trees. This was the case at Anaa, but at Kaukura, another island in the group, it not only destroyed houses and trees, but many lives were lost. It is reported that there were between eighty and a hundred men, women, and children who were swallowed up in the depths of the sea, and it is believed by some that many of them could have been saved had they remained on land and taken to the trees, but the natives thought there was more safety in going inside the lagoon in their little boats, but in doing this they with their crafts went down. It is related by George Richmond, a white man living there now, and who was there at the time of the disaster, that he saved his life and that of his wife by lashing himself and her to a cocoanut tree, thereby hindering the waves from sweeping them into the sea, and at the same time permitting them to get their breath during the interval of time when the waves would go down.

It was during this time that the Saints' meeting house at Otepipi was destroyed and in their attempt to rebuild it they were again arrested and taken before the Governor. After threatening them and in almost every way trying to get them to quit praying and preaching, they were again set at liberty. But the Saints on Anaa were not alone in receiving punishment and persecution for their belief. Elder Brown relates that on his last mission to the Islands ('92 and '93) he learned of some of the persecutions the Saints on Raivavai and Tubuai were subjected to. The first named island is where the natives prepared a fire to burn him, which was described in one of our former articles. Brother Brown thus describes it: "During my late stay on Tubuai I learned that after I left Raivavai in 1852, the Protestants commenced a crusade upon the Saints of that island. After punishing them in various ways they stripped them naked and put them bound in an open boat and took them to Tubuai, ninety-five or a hundred miles to the west. Then they said they had rid their island of Mormonism. This fanned the flame of intolerance on Tubuai, and they said that as the Missionaries had left there, their disciples must renounce their religion or leave this land. So they imprisoned some, sent some to Tahiti, fined others, and finally hung several of the leaders by the heels for some time with only their heads and shoulders resting on the dirt floor, and they were only released when a white man called there with his vessel and told the promoters of the cruelty, that he would report it to the French Government at once and would see that the men and women were set at liberty and their persecutors severely punished for their cruel acts. They afterwards received word from Tahiti that the prisoners they had sent there had been set at liberty and the action of their accusers condemned by the French authorities."

With this article we present the last Tahitian picture that we have for the present. It represents some of the natives going through one of their exercises during the celebration on the 14th of July. This being a great day with the French the natives gather together at Papeete and have a time of drinking, carousing, and engaging in various sports. Many costumes are made for the occasion from the bark of trees, etc., while others of the girls and women don their mother-hubbards of white, and the boys or men their black trousers and white shirts. During this celebration boat, canoe, and swimming races are indulged in, and also diving. Singing contests are also held and the competing company that can make the most noise is generally recognized as the best. It is, however, due to the natives to state that they as a class are singers, and many of them possess voices that are not harsh for the ear to listen to. In their singing in Church all, as a rule, join together, from the gray-haired grand-father and mother down to the boy and girl of eight and ten years of age.

Eugene M. Cannon.
(TO BE CONTINUED.)

WHEN you have found your talent, do not despise it or be disappointed in it or yourself because you have not some other; but honor it, respect it, make the best of it even if it is not much of a gift.

A WISE and good man will turn examples of all sorts to his advantage. The good he will make his patterns, and strive to equal or excel them. The bad he will by all means avoid.

A DAUGHTER OF THE NORTH.

Politics and Coffee.

No. IV.

(CONTINUED FROM PAGE 220.)

"COME, Atelie, sit down, let Olga serve the coffee" said Captain Heldman. "Steen has something to say which you wish to hear."

Atelie dropped into a chair at the end of the table around which Hr. Steen, Hr. Larsen and her father were sitting. She placed her elbows on the table and her chin between her hands. With a roguish smile she prepared to listen.

The parlor of Heimstad House presented a cozy scene that evening. The big lamp was lighted, the blinds were drawn, and the table shone with silver and china. The Captain felt well and was in a talkative mood. Hr. Steen was as jovial as could be expected of a politician just before an uncertain election. Hr. Larsen—well, he had no cause for complaint. It was not often that he was the guest of such people as Captain and Froken Heldman.

"Well?" said Atelie, thinking the pause rather long.

"I see that Steen is reluctant" said the Captain. "He thinks, Atelie, that we should do something to check this wild, nonsensical talk about the Blue Bird, which, he claims, is injuring his chances of election."

"I simply want the truth to be known. A statement from you in *Portere* might help. I know, Atelie, that you are not anxious to see me elected, but you certainly would not do anything unfair to defeat me."

"Defeat you, Steen? What do you mean? Why should Atelie object to you going to Storlinget? She is a more pronounced Radical than you are."

Atelie sat upright. She did not like Hr. Steen exposing her that way.

Hr. Steen saw it, and tried, in a way, to smoothe things over.

"Steen," said she, "you know its all foolishness this blaming you for the accident to our boat, but if a statement from us will do you any good, I'll write one tonight and send to *Portere* in the morning."

"Well, folks," said Steen good-naturedly, "my chances are not any too good as it is, and anything that might help me will be thankfully accepted."

"Well," said the Captain," we'll do that, though you know my opinion on your views."

Here Olga brought the coffee, and cups were soon clattering in unison to the small talk of the company. The Captain did his share both in drinking coffee and in talking. He explained how he had insisted on his wife sitting at the same table with him, even when they had company, and denounced the custom in some families of making the wife simply a servant when there were visitors. When she had died two years ago, Atelie had taken her place and followed the order he had instituted.

"I learned a few lessons in America, Hr. Larsen," said he, "but among them was not a wholesome respect for your politics."

"The system can not be blamed for the abuse of power by officials," said Hr. Steen.

"I know a tree by its fruits. It is true that I have not closely studied the government of the United States, but I have had some experience with American politicians, and I say that many of them are tricksters whose sole aim is to receive the spoils of office."

"What do you think of that, Hr. Larsen?" asked Atelie of that gentleman who had been listening to the others without taking any part in the conversation.

"Well, I am compelled to admit that there is a great deal of truth in what your father says, but of course—"

"Of course, Larsen, you will uphold a government that allows full sway to a set of rogues. No; gentlemen, I am satisfied with what we have. King Oscar and Storlinget are good enough for me."

"I fear, father, that you are losing all your northern patriotism," said his daughter.

"No; I am not. I love the old fatherland as well as any of you; I love the order which here prevails; I love the justice which is meted out to all alike; I love this government's honesty and stability."

"You see" remarked Hr. Steen to Hr. Larsen, "Captain Heldman is a staunch Loyalist. He has sailed under the union flag so long, that it would be impossible for him to change. All we ask is what the constitution allows us, and among that we claim is that we should have our own representatives abroad in the consulate service. We are now represented by Sweden. The value of Sweden's shipping is insignificant when compared with that of Norway. Storlinget has repeatedly asked for justice on this point, but the king and his Swedish ministers have refused."

"That is a question which should be settled in a united council but the Radical Storlinget has refused," snorted the Captain.

"We claim also, Hr. Larsen," continued Steen not noticing the last remark, "that Norway is able to take care of her own affairs."

"You are revolutionists and your ultimate aim is to overthrow the government and make Norway a republic.

Steen, answer me that, if it isn't true?"

"And what if it is?"

"There, Atelie, publish that in tomorrow's *Portere* by the side of your statement," at which the whole company laughed.

"We have an ideal country for a republic." Steen continued. "Our people, inspired by mountain and sea are liberty loving. Our children are getting an education equal to any in the world. The ballot will not be in ignorant hands. We are able to govern ourselves without the aid of kings, and I say that we should have the chance. We will too, some day."

"Atelie, let's have some more coffee," said the Captain. He was supplied and then he withdrew to his own room. Atelie cleared the table, then sat down again with her crochet work.

"Yes, Hr. Larsen, we need a change in this country. We are not free, in many ways. Church and State are one. One only, out of the many religious denominations of our land, has a fair chance. The king, members of his cabinet, judges, school teachers, and many other public officers must belong to the Lutheran Church. Thus religion is nothing but a policy cloak in many instances. Your own religion, Hr. Larsen, is by law placed with the Mohammedan and you are really not lawfully allowed to promulgate it here. The public opinion of a liberty-loving people alone makes the law a dead letter. Again, take for instance the divisions of our executive department. It consists of a prime minister and six members which are the heads of the various departments. They are all appointed by the king and are responsible only to him, and he is responsble to nobody."

"What are these departments," asked Hr. Larsen.

"The church, the justice, the interior, public works, finance, war, and the auditing departments. Now see what a picture this cabinet makes under certain conditions. The head of the church department has to do with all religious matters. The head of the finance department has to do with the adjustment of revenues. He must, for example, calculate just how much whisky shall be made, and the tax on it. Now do you see the picture? The same body of men deciding how much and what kind of religion, and how much and what kinds of whisky will be best for the people of the kingdom of Norway."

Captain Heldman had finished his pipe and come in to say good night.

"You've converted Hr. Larsen have you, Steen? Well, there's no harm been done, Hr. Larsen's isn't a voter. Good night, gentlemen. You must leave tonight, Steen? You might as well remain until tomorrow. You won't gain any more votes tonight."

"I have a meeting to attend tomorrow, and I must catch the eleven o'clock boat. I'm sorry but—"

"Good night then, I must to bed."

"Atelie," said Steen, "you have a good old father, even if he is odd."

"I think so. You had better have a little more lunch before you leave."

"Not another bit, please. Larsen, which way do you go?"

"I am going to make a tour of Telemarken, and expect to start tomorrow."

"I wish you success, but those fellows up there are hard to get out of ruts. 'What was good enough for our fathers is good enough for us' is their argument." He looked at his watch. "It is half past ten. I think I had better be going."

"Then, I'll say good-night too, "said

Hr. Larsen, "I must get an early start in the morning."

"We'll go down to the wharf with you, Steen. Will you go along Hr. Larsen?"

The latter had no objection. His offer to retire was solely for the benefit of the other two. Now he got his hat and they all three sauntered slowly down the dark road to the water. The steamer soon came along, aglow with light. Hr. Steen sprang lightly aboard, and as the boat steamed off he waved his hat to the two on the shore. "Hr. Steen is a fine man," said Hr. Larsen as they turned up the road again.

"Yes; his soul is in politics just now, and it will go hard with him if he is defeated."

The road was quite dark. Everything was still at that late hour, and the evening breeze could be heard in the tops of the pines singing a soft, solemn strain.

"Was our talk very tiresome to you this evening," she asked.

"Indeed, it was quite interesting," said he.

"But you did'nt get a chance to say a word."

"Why should I? I don't want to preach all the time, I assure you."

They got nearly to the house before either spoke again. Then he asked:

"Did you read the last book I left you?"

"I have'nt completed it yet. This racing business has upset me, but now I shall finish it. Father has read it long ago and is ready for more. He was wondering yesterday if you didn't want to hold some meetings in the house."

"You are all so kind, Froken Held-man, that I can not thank you enough. I don't think it would be wise to hold meetings here just at present. You know, we must be wise as well as harmless."

"Perhaps you are right; but don't fail to call whenever you come this way. Goodnight. Don't leave in the morning before you get your breakfast, and I think father would like to see you before you go. Good-night."

She held out her hand and he pressed it lightly.

"Good-night," said he.

(TO BE CONTINUED.)

THE ANGELS COME AGAIN!

How oft we have lingered o'er stories of old,
　　When angels of God were to favored ones sent;
With feelings enlisted, we read, or were told,
　　Their mission and ministry yet were unspent.

Though strangers for ages to man they have been,
　　No welcome was theirs on earth's sin-covered sod;
Yet worked they as faithful, if long, long unseen,
　　In the cause of salvation, the Priesthood of God!

The guests of the Prophets and worthies of old,
　　On errands important, as light they have run;
They flash to the earth from the gates made of gold,
　　Through space as far distant as sun is to sun!

As teachers, revealing the truth most sublime,
　　Or telling the destiny nations must feel;
In Prophets rebuking the sins of their time,
　　Then stooping to succor, or sad heart to heal!

In Bethlehem singing, in prison, to ope',
　　'Mid flame and red death by the martyrs they stood;
When chained, or in dungeons, 'mid wild beasts to cope,
　　'Twas Angels gave patience in baptism of blood!

The world shut the door on their visit at last,
　　It needed not wisdom,—at least, such as theirs;
So ages of night went reluctantly past,
　　Thick darkness of Egypt, the world had to bear.

As dreams of the past, until ages fled by,
　　Man wandered in error, and wrestled in pain,
And then there came down from the rifted blue sky,
　　The Angels of God, to the earth once again!

When Joseph, the boy, was for converse prepared,
　　The Lord of the Angels, just opened the way;
The pathway (man broken) again was repaired,
　　For they visit—are seen, since that glorified day.

They minister freely to "heirs of salvation,
That still is their mission, their labor of love,
And Gospel believers of every nation,
May feel their sweet presence from mansions above.

Come nations, exult in the sunlight of old,
Ye meek ones arise, in the name of your King,
More welcome this news, than are mountains of gold,
It peals through these valleys, the mountain tops ring.

The theme is Salvation, the Gospel made plain,
The Priesthood to guide us, as in the old way;
'Tis music to millions, 'tis light without strain,
There's the fire of the Gods, in its life-giving ray!

Hail, hail, with a shout of thanksgiving to God,
The Angel appointed the end to bring in,
When earth shall be cleansed, and no more on its sod
The devil be found, or the dark seas of sin!
        H. W. Naisbitt.

HISTORICAL ENGLAND.

London.
No V.
(CONTINUED FROM PAGE 208.)

To write a history of London would be a stupendous task. A complete history of London even during the last half century would in itself necessitate the compilation of a small library. To undertake to write a history of the great metropolis since its foundation and subsequent growth, would be to expend years in historical research and possibly after its completion it would be voted exceedingly dry and uninteresting.

However, I will try in this short article to pick out a few prominent incidents that are intimately associated with that historical city; and which may be of interest to the boys and girls of Utah, a great many of whom came from England, or are descended from those who did.

To give an account of the origin of London, is in itself a hopeless undertaking, for the best historians differ widely on that subject and further as to the date, which is of such antiquity as to be lost. Geoffrey of Monmouth, an old writer, claims it was founded by Brutus, nephew of the famous Aneas, and was called New Troy, and that at length it was walled by King Lud, when it obtained the name of Caer Lud or Lud's town; upon this supposition some historians go to the length of computing that it had its origin 1107 years before Christ, 600 years before the capture of Babylon by the Medes and Persians mentioned in Daniel v. 31., and 350 years before Rome was built. Others suppose that this city derived the name of London from the British words Llwyn, a wood, and Dinas, a town, signifying a town in a wood, others again claim that it is derived from the British Lhong, a ship, and Dinas, a town, as it is a conceded fact that even before the birth of Christ it was a trading place, or mart of the British trade with the Phoenicians, Greeks and Gauls. Such are some of the theories advanced of the world's metropolis. Be that as it may London possessed no brick or stone buildings until after the occupation by the Romans; for the ancient Britons were very modest about their dwelling places, and inhabited huts built of wattle work, willows, etc., the whole being plastered over with mud. However, Tacitus observes that "in the year 26 Londium was very famous for the multitude of its merchants and the greatness of its traffic." Soon after this Suetonius abandoned the city to the fury of the British Princess Boadicea, because it was too large to be successfully defended by his little army of 10,000 Roman soldiers, which is decidedly a proof of its being, even at that date, of considerable extent.

Boadicea subsequently captured the

city, burnt it and put everyone therein to the sword.

London was not occupied by the Romans to any extent until three centuries later, when they built a wall around it—a small part of which still stands and is carefully preserved near Aldgate. After this period London began to assume a position in history. The Britons, Danes, and the Normans all occupied it on various occasions accompanied with deeds of blood and fire.

Probably hundreds of Mormon Elders have made their exit from Cannon Street Station (the terminus of the South Eastern Railway) and have never given the Church of St. Swithin's across the street a passing glance. If they did it is still more probable that a stone protected by an iron screen, and built into the wall of the church escaped their notice. This stone is none other than the Roman milliarium stone, or central point used by them from which to measure distances, a survey beacon in fact. There this stone has stood for centuries (or to be more correct it has been moved some feet from its original site) a silent witness of numerous stirring scenes by fire, sword, pestilence, change of monarchies and dynasties; there seems to have been a certain superstition connected with this piece of rock, judging by the way certain leaders of rebellions, Wat Tyler, and Perkin Warbeck to wit, would stroll up to this stone, strike it with their swords, and swear rash oaths over it.

After the Norman Conquest, 1066, William Duke of Normandy, or as he was called William I, made London his headquarters; and it is from this that the city began to make huge strides towards being really a city; for the Normans seemed to have a penchant for building. William caused the Tower to be built—of which we will say more in another number, also many monasteries and churches in London, and to this day, the distinctive style of Norman architecture is very much in evidence throughout the south of England.

During the reign of Henry II London began to achieve an unenviable notoriety from the fact that none, unless he were a baron or noble with armed escorts at his command, was safe from the depredations of robbers and bands of marauders that infested the streets, and even attacked the houses of the wealthy, plundering the same and murdering the occupants; however, the king caused some of these robbers to be captured and brought to trial; one of the ringleaders was found to be John the Olde "a citizen of good standing and credit," who promptly offered the king 500 marks in consideration that his life be spared. Henry (after the good old custom of those days) found out where the money could be found, annexed the same, and promptly executed the owner, after which the city became more quiet. However, on the day before the coronation of Richard I (commonly called the "lion heart" on account of his bravery in battle) some fourteen years later, 1189, a dreadful massacre of the Jews occurred in this city. Intimation had been given to that despised people not to appear at the ceremony; but many endeavoring to satisfy their curiosity, carried presents to the king and endeavored to gain access to the Abbey Church at Westminster, but being expelled by the royal servants, a rumor spread among the mob, that is always present when any great celebrations are to be viewed, that the king had given orders for the entire destruction of the Jews, whereupon the rabble fell upon these poor defenceless Hebrews and butchered them in cold blood. The mob having tasted blood, rushed to the city, plundered and burnt the Jewish quarter and murdered men, women and children, committing horrible atrocities.

About this time the citizens dug a deep ditch (200 feet wide and 30 feet deep) around the city wall, which as may be estimated was a huge undertaking in those days of primative tools. Further a great many houses were built within the city, the old ones being pulled down and large and more commodious ones being erected in their stead; these were plastered and whitewashed. The people further petitioned the king to prohibit the burning of sea coal, within the city as it blackened and spoiled the buildings. Sea coal be it understood was coal washed up by the waves, as coal mining was not then in existence.

We will pass by the plague, the execution of Sir William Wallace in London, Wat Tyler's Rebellion, the wars of the Roses and other historical events, and come down to the reign of Henry VIII, that monarch that has been such a puzzle to students of human character, who ascended the throne in 1509 at the age of nineteen. He gave promise of making a good king and was a general favorite, being endowed with comely manners and possessed of a handsome face and figure. About this time Martin Luther in Germany was defying the church of Rome and throwing some light upon their practices and creed in general. Henry subsequently wrote a book on the seven sacraments, which was a violent attack upon the heresies of Luther. This book was presented with great ceremony by a special ambassador to Pope Leo X. who rewarded the royal author with the title of Defender of the Faith, which title is still held by the monarchs of England and to this day the letters F. D. appear upon all British coins; the Pope further sent the king an autograph letter in which he praised "his wisdom, learning, zeal, charity, gravity, gentleness and meekness," most of which epithets few people could have less deserved.

Henry, however, had an object in view, viz., that of ultimately raising his favorite Cardinal Wolsey to the Papal chair. The following year the Pope died and Adrain VI was elected in his place to the great mortification of Henry and his cardinal. Up to this time the king had been married four times, his first wife having died, while his second "sweet Anne Boleyn" was beheaded within the Tower on a trumped up charge, he marrying Jane Seymour the day after the brutal execution, she subsequently died, and now Henry found himself married to a lady whose picture Cardinal Wolsey had presented to him for inspection. It seems that the artists even in those days were not above flattering their studies, and when Henry met his proposed bride he was very much chagrined to find how ugly she was. However, he married her and at once began to repent having done so, and cast around for a means of getting rid of her. A young priest named Cranmer of the advanced school and follower of Luther to some extent vaguely hinted at divorce, but this was an abomination in the sight of the church of Rome not to be tolerated. Headstrong Harry promptly seized the bull by the horns and cut himself and England adrift from the blighting influence of the Church of Rome, obtained the required divorce and married twice again before he died, one more of his wives Catherine Howard being put out of the way by the headsman's axe on a trumped up charge of treason. Thus we can see from what source the Reformation in England obtained a firm footing.

Wickliffe's opinions of two hundred years previous—notwithstanding the early persecutions of his followers who had been burnt, broken on the wheel, and undergone terrible and unspeakable torments for their belief—had never been eradicated, and the Lollards as they were called had slowly but surely increased in numbers, and in the early part of this reign their opinions and numbers had gained renewed strength from the success of their Protestant friends in Germany under Martin Luther. Henry VIII at first persecuted these Lollards terribly, and many were the fires that blazed around London cremating alive these poor seekers after light in those dark days. But upon the king quarreling with the Pope there was a change, these persecutions were relaxed, while the Roman Catholics began to come in for their share of un welcome attention; but still England was far from coming out of the darkness and superstition of Popery and the legends of centuries. Henry's character and actions were made up of strange opposites. He abolished all monasteries around London and confiscated to his own private purse the jewels, gold and silver wealth and rents connected with them; he forbade the worship of images, commanded the services to be read in English and not in Latin as heretofore, and yet he burnt many creatures for heresy. He caused the Bible to be translated and then only allowed authorized people to read it, and then only certain portions. His son Edward VI with the assistance of Cranmer on the death of Henry VIII took up the work of the Reformation. In his reign the Book of Common Prayer as used in the church of England was published (1549) together with the 42 articles (subsequently reduced to 39) and church catechism were compiled. All images, statues, stained glass windows in churches in London and England; by order of the king, were destroyed and . removed) an act of vandalism to be deeply regretted from an archaelogical standpoint) many are the roofless ruined walls dotted throughout England, monuments of Edward's zeal, where once stood stately abbeys and monasteries. A number of them were sold to noblemen for country seats and still retain their old names and legends.

Latimer was appointed the king's preacher. The young monarch had a pulpit erected in the Royal Gardens in London, where Edward would sit in the shade, while Latimer would preach to his congregation of half a dozen, sermons of four or five hours' duration. Edward was essentially a student and loved learning, he founded and endowed Christ's Hospital, Newgate Street, London, commonly known as the "blue coat school" from the fact that the thousands of boys who receive their education there still dress in the costume of four hundred years ago. It is quite a source of surprise for a stranger to look upon one of these school boys dressed as he is in a long blue tunic or coat reaching to the heels, a pair of vivid yellow stockings, velvet knee breeches, ponderous thick low cut shoes, a leather belt around the waist fastened by a silver buckle and minus a hat—no matter how inclement the weather; the bluecoat boy never wears any head gear except rough hair. The color of their stockings never fails to elicit the query from the omnipresent London street arab "Yah! who dipped his leg in a mustard pot?" The boys further retain a great many of their old customs and visit the Lord Mayor of London at the Mansion House in state once a year, when he gravely presents each boy with a new shilling (some of the seniors a guinea) together with a bunch of raisins, which in the days of Edward was considered to be no mean gift. In this reign London was granted a liberal charter and the Lord Mayor, aldermen and citizens received lands and tenements in Southwalk (then a suburb). Edward going the way of all flesh, his sister Mary took the reins of government and promptly set to work to once more establish the power of the Roman church and the Pope in England. Latimer and Cranmer were burned at the stake for their religious opinions. Within three years nearly as many hundred prominent people were burned publicly, while the number of those who suffered indescribable and fiendish tortures, imprisonment and fines for their belief were legion. However, upon the death of "Bloody Mary" as historians call her, her sister Elizabeth (good Queen Bess) was proclaimed queen, 1558. At this time by far the greater portion of London was contained within massive walls, the city being approached through gates defended by portcullis and drawbridges.

Geo. E. Carpenter.

[TO BE CONTINUED.]

PREFER what is good of a lower or inferior work or material to what is bad of a higher work or material; for this is the way to improve every kind of work, and to put every kind of material to better use.

KINDNESS is the music of good will to men; and on this harp the smallest fingers may play Heaven's sweetest tunes on earth.

O'ER THE OCEAN.

O'ER the hills and rugged mountains,
    O'er the broad and dusty plain,
Over deep and gurgling rivers,
    Far across the mighty main;
By the holy angels guarded,
    Comes the welcome news today,
Zion's sons are safely landed,
    O'er the ocean, far away.

Now with rapturous thanksgiving,
    Is a father's pulses stirred,
While he bendeth low, and utters
    Some deep, heartfelt, grateful word;
That his son has been protected,
    That the voice he did obey,
Which had called him to a nation,
    O'er the ocean, far away.

Now are calm eyes raised to heaven,
    And a tear would seem to start,
But is quickly checked and folded
    In a mother's thankful heart;
And she feels her anxious watchings,
    God will more than all repay,
In the one that's true and worthy
    O'er the ocean, far away.

Brothers, joyous, proud and happy,
    Hear, and many a prayer ascends
With the thought, " They, for the Gospel,
    Left their Utah homes and friends! "
Sisters, in their joy forgetful
    Of the weary, long delay,
Pray God speed and safe returning,
    O'er the ocean, far away.

Now and then a faithful fond one,
    Eager grasps the precious news,
None may watch the glad eyes sparkle,
    Or the fresh cheek's changing hues,
But good angels smile and pencil,
    While a maiden's pure lips pray,
For her brave young missionary,
    O'er the ocean, far away.

And for others wives and children
    Gather 'round the quiet hearth;
Some with secret prayers and blessings,
    Some with songs of heartfelt mirth;
Oh ! the thought of home must brighten
    Faith and hope with glor'ous ray,
To the faithful missionary,
    O'er the ocean, far away.

L. L. Greene Richards.

FOUR MORMON GIRLS.

A Story of Twenty Years Ago.

(CONTINUED FROM PAGE 216.)

JEAN had been esatblished in her new school for about six months and was getting on splendidly, making an excellent reputation as a teacher.

She had been fortunate in obtaining a good boarding place at Bishop Johnson's and their kind and thoughtful treatment of her had done much to ward off the attacks of homesickness which were natural to a girl who had never been so long away from home and, separated from all her kindred before.

It was Saturday, and various savory odors pervaded the Bishop's sunny kitchen, as his wife and daughers bustled about preparing the Sunday dinner; for they were expecting Elder X. and other missionaries to speak to them at their conference on the morrow, and a spiritual as well as a temporal feast was anticipated.

Jean had never seen Elder X. but, like the heroes of old, his fame had preceded him, and the accounts of the stirling qualities of mind and heart, which had early in life raised him to a position of responsibility and prominence in the Church, caused her to regard him with a sort of hero-worship, and she could hardly wait for tomorrow to come.

She had insisted on helping Sister Johnson, (for Saturdays were her "blue days" unless she was able to keep her self fully occupied) and, pretty well tired out, had retired to bed and to sleep.

The morning sun shining in her face awakened her with a start, and she lay, with her head pillowed on her rounded arm, and her blue eyes fixed on the distant, snowy mountain tops, trying to recall the beautiful dream, the happy influence of which still pervaded her senses.

"Ah, yes!" and the memory of it rushed into her mind like strains of long-forgotten music.

She had dreamed that she was at home in her father's house, with youth, and love, and life before her, and that a man came to ask her own, and her parents' consent to her union with him.

He was a stranger, years older than herself she knew, for the wavy brown hair which was brushed back from the beautiful forehead was streaked with silver, but she had loved him instantly with a pure and fervent devotion; and the knowledge that he fully reciprocated her feelings, caused such a sense of security and restfulness to pervade her entire being, as to far surpass anything she had ever experienced.

They sat together side by side in happy conversation, and he had drawn from his pocket a gold neck chain, of fine and exquisite workmanship, and said:

"See, I have brought a present for you." They examined it together and he pointed out to her its varied beauties, and then clasped it lovingly about her neck.

He then called her attention to a parcel laying on a chair near by, saying: "I have brought this for you, too, but I am almost sorry I did so for I am afraid you will not like it." She saw that it was a black dress pattern, and it seemed to be of coarse and flimsy texture and she was indeed disappointed, but tried to hide her real feelings, lest she should wound him.

"To prove to you how much better I love you than I have ever loved any one else," she playfully said to him, "I, who have always made it a rule never to accept presents from gentlemen, though I have had several opportunities of doing so, now accept this from you."

Her joking did not in the least deceive him as to her true feelings, and after a pause, he said:

"Come, let us examine it more closely, I think I can point out beauties you have failed to notice."

They walked to where the parcel was lying and handled and examined it, and she discovered that it was really beautiful, and so expressed herself.

They again sat down and he told her of his family, of his wives and his children, but not one pang of jealousy smote her heart; and they were still conversing blissfully together when she awoke.

"Now I wonder what can be the meaning of that vivid dream," she mused as she hastily dressed herself. There was little time for speculation, however, for she could hear the clatter of dishes being put on the table for breakfast and the Bishop telling the bcys to hitch up in time for the 9:45 train, on which the missionaries were expected.

"Will you favor us, Miss Stuart, by playing the organ this morning at meeting? Our organist has just sent word that she is sick," the Bishop said to her, as she bid him good morning, and she readily consented.

The meeting house was crowded and Jean at her post was waiting to begin, when the missionaries arrived; and she could hear the pleasant greetings among the brethren on the stand, but the organ was placed directly in front and facing the pulpit, which compelled her to sit with her back to the speakers throughout the entire services, the crowded condition of the room making it impossible for her to shift her position.

It was quite a disappointment to her,

not to be able to see as well as hear the speakers, but she enjoyed the speaking nevertheless, and the golden truths which flowed in eloquent and impassioned sentences from the inspired lips of Elder X. made a deep impression upon her. At the close of the sermon, the chorister placed the anthem they were to sing upon the music rack for her, and she saw that it was the same one which Rintha and Jamie had sung under her window on that memorable night so long ago.

A flood of memories swept over her, but she set her teeth to still the trembling of her fingers, pouring into the deep, solemn tones of the instrument her gratitude for deliverance from the thralldom of an unfortunate love and her sorrow for the unhappy fate of the darling sister.

The congregation rose to their feet and she bowed her head reverently during the benediction, and when the final "amen" was pronounced, raised her beautiful face, pale with emotion, and gazed straight into the eyes of Elder X. and with a great throb of her heart, almost painful in its intensity, instantly recognized the face of the hero of her dream, whose speaking eyes now smiled back at her a mutual recognition.

How she got out of the house and back into her own room she never knew, but there was a dim remembrance of the pleasant greetings of friends and her vague replies. She bowed her head in gratitude to God, that He had given her another glorious testimony of His power and goodness, and the beautiful words of the psalm welled up to her fervent lips:

"Bless the Lord, Oh my soul; and all that is within me bless His holy name. Who redeemeth thy life from destruction, who crowneth thee with loving kindness and tender mercies."

"Who was that young lady at the organ?" questioned Elder X. of the Bishop as they were going home to dinner.

"That is our new school teacher Miss Stuart of N—."

"She is a fine musician, and you have a very good choir."

The Bishop introduced the missionaries to his family, including Miss Stuart, and Elder X. improved the opportunity of cultivating her acquaintance.

Before he left the town he inquired of her as to the probable date of her return home, and asked permission to call upon her and her parents, to which last question she gave her assent.

Three years ago I spent some months in one of our temple cities where Douglas and Rintha reside, and we had a most enjoyable visit together.

I found her occupying every moment she could spare from her husband and children, performing the vast work in the temple promised her in her blessing.

We get a flying glimpse of our bonny Jean occasionally, but she has been an exile for conscience sake for many years (which she interprets as the black dress of her dream).

Of course the law would allow her now to return, but she is attached to the home of her exile and prefers to remain where she is. That she is happy in the love of her noble husband, her bright face and sparkling eyes are a sure index, and that she has one of the loveliest families of children I have ever seen I can of a surety testify.

Chatty has never married again and is still her father's housekeeper, and a model one, too.

She is beginning to get considerably interested in politics and has developed quite a talent for stump speaking.

And Jamie? Well, I don't mind telling you that I married him, myself.

Sarah E. Pearson.

A PLEASANT STORY OF NAPOLEON.

PLEASANT stories of Napoleon I, are exceedingly scarce, but here is one. The French Colonel Varennes had written several confidential letters to a pretended friend, in which he censured Napoleon about some military actions. The pretended friend, expecting a good reward by promotion or otherwise, sent the letter to the Emperor. Varennes was summoned before him. Napoleon showed him what he had received, and asked sternly:

"Are you not ashamed of these letters?"

"No, sire," he replied, "but I am ashamed of the address from which the letters last came."

Napoleon's manner brightened, and he said:

"You are right. Your communications to your pretended friend were confidential, but he has played the traitor on you. But if in the future you want to subject my orders to criticism you ought to send your opinion to a better address; that is to say, to myself, and I hereby appoint you a member of my Council of War."

The pretended friend was transferred to a subordinate position far away on the frontier of the empire.

IDLENESS is the mother of many wanton children. They that do nothing are in the ready way to do worse than nothing.

✤ ✤ THE ✤ ✤
Juvenile Instructor

GEORGE Q. CANNON, EDITOR.

SALT LAKE CITY, UTAH, APRIL 15, 1897.

EDITORIAL THOUGHTS.

GIVE THE LORD THE GLORY.

THE Lord, through the mouth of the Prophet Hosea, compared Israel to a woman who had been unfaithful to her first husband, and had gone after other lovers, and who said, "I will go after my lovers, that give me my bread and my water, my wool and my flax, my oil and my drink." And the Lord said:

"She shall follow after her lovers, but she shall not overtake them; and she shall seek them, but shall not find them: then shall she say, I will go and return to my first husband; for then was it better with me than now.

"For she did not know that I gave her corn, and wine, and oil, and multiplied her silver and gold, which they prepared for Baal."

There was an important lesson conveyed to Israel in these statements—a lesson, too, which we who live in the present day may find profitable.

There is not that disposition in many quarters that there should be to give glory to the Lord for the blessings which have been bestowed upon us since coming to this land. When the Latter-day Saints came to this country, nothing seemed more unlikely than that this should become a fertile land. The Prophet Brigham (and others who had the spirit of prophecy) saw what the country would become; but the bulk of the people did not conceive of the prosperity which has attended the settlement and labors of the people in these valleys. It is true that those who were teachers and leaders of the people at that time spoke very hopefully of the future and of the many favors which God would show unto His people in modifying the climate, in increasing the water, in taking away from the land its poisonous elements, and making it a fertile land. President Brigham Young was especially inspired to speak in this strain unto the Saints, and his discourses in the early days were full of promises and were inspiring in hopefulness in encouraging the people in the midst of the distresses and privations which then had to be met. It required faith, however, on the part of those who heard those prophecies and encouraging words to believe they would ever be fulfilled. The faith of some failed and they in a year or two left the valley for California.

Could the people have seen then that which we see now, they would have been overpowered with a feeling of thankfulness. They would have thought that any one who would not see the hand of the Lord in all this and look upon it as an exhibition of His miraculous power, must be very blind, and hard of heart, and unthankful; for they knew that nothing but the blessing of the Lord could effect such wonderful changes as we now witness.

———

A new generation, however, has grown up since those days—a generation not familiar with the early conditions; a generation whose knowledge of the situation at that time is dependent upon that which they have been told. There is danger, under these circumstances, of there being a failure to realize how wonderfully great have been the blessings that have been bestowed upon the people, and how they should adore the God of heaven for having brought them about. It is without doubt God's favor, and in fulfillment of His promises, that the change and happy condition of physical affairs which we now witness has been brought to pass. It has not been man, nor man's power, that has done it. It is true, man has been the instrument; man has labored, planned; but it has been the Lord that has crowned those labors and those plans with the success which has resulted. As in the case of ancient Israel, the bread and the water, the wine, and the corn, and the oil, and the wool, the silver and the gold, have been the gifts of the Lord. They have not come from any other source. No false gods have brought about this wonderful change.

The hearts of the Latter-day Saints should always be turned to the true God, the God of heaven, whose worship has been restored to us, and whose promises we see so abundantly fulfilled. It has been by His power that this climate has been modified. It has been by His blessing that the water has been increased, that the soil has been made so fruitful, and that all the labors of the people have been crowned with such abundant success. It is through that power also that the silver and the gold have been multiplied in this land. And we should never forget it.

It was the custom among the children of Israel, when they were living righteous lives and serving God faithfully, to constantly remind their offspring of the mighty works which the Lord had performed in leading their ancestors out of Egypt, in delivering them at the Red Sea, in preserving them in their journey in the wilderness, and guiding them in safety to the land which the Lord had promised to their father Abraham. It was considered a proper thing for the rising generation to have these great works of the Lord and deliverances impressed upon their memories, that they might have constantly in mind the Lord's power and His ability to fulfill His promises. One of the prophets, in alluding to the mighty works that should be performed in the last days, mentions this fact, that the children of Israel had cherished the remembrance of those mighty works which were wrought in behalf of Israel when the Lord delivered them from the bondage in Egypt. The Book of Mormon also contains frequent allusions to those great events.

In like manner it is the duty of the Latter-day Saints to instruct their children concerning the great works which the Lord has performed in our day for our salvation. They should be dwelt upon. Every child should be taught concerning these events, and should be shown the manner in which the Lord has fulfilled the promises which He made to His people in our day.

It would be a fine object lesson to point out to the children of our Sunday Schools to the barren wastes which surround us, bring home to their attention how all this land looked when the Lord led His servant Brigham and his associates to it; to point out to them the alkali lands, and how difficult it was to subdue them; to impress upon them that there was a time in the valleys—in the early settlement—when fruit trees were cut down by frost, and it appeared as though they never could flourish here; and describe to them those conditions which existed which made it seem as if this land would always be a country without comfort, a country undesirable, a country in which it would be difficult for men and women to live, except by the hardest and most severe toil, a country where comforts could not be multiplied, and which appeared as though, through its hardships and privations, it would eat up its inhabitants. For these were the existing conditions for many years after the Latter-day Saints were led to this land, and to all human appearance, they were not likely to ever change.

It required faith to believe that Utah could ever be a desirable place in which to live. There was nothing here to invite them to stay contentedly, except the knowledge that the Lord had appointed this place as a resting place for them—a place where they should live until perhaps they should receive instructions to build up the centre stake of Zion. They were prepared in coming here to endure all privations and to encounter all difficulties that might lie in their pathway, because they felt that it was the will of the Lord that this should be their abiding place. The Lord made promises to them concerning the blessings he had in store for them and the prosperity which awaited them. But to every person who looked at the surroundings with the natural eye, these appeared very remote.

Our children should be impressed with all this. Parents should take pains to teach them, so that they will see in all the gifts that we enjoy—in the "bread and the corn, the wool and the oil, the silver and the gold—" the hand of God and the fulfillment of His promises to His people; that they will not attribute this to other gods, or to other causes, but will see the hand of the Great Creator, the God whom we worship, the God who has founded the Church of Jesus Christ of Latter-day Saints, and give constant glory and praises to Him therefor.

The Lord has shown by His revelations that He desires His people to be a healthy, vigorous people. A careful perusal of the revelations which He has given to this Church gives proof of this. The laws which He revealed to ancient Israel, also, bear abundant evidence of the great interest which our Heavenly Father takes in His children and in their welfare.

Good health, therefore, should be sought for by the Latter-day Saints. The counsels which the Lord has given to the people as to the best method of living in order to be healthy and strong should be practiced with care. The daily lives of the people should exhibit their respect for God's word.

A healthy man or a healthy woman, all other things being equal, can accomplish much more than a weakly and unhealthy man or woman. A missionary who goes out to the nations full of bodily vigor is likely to also possess mental vigor, and he can accomplish more in his mission than a man can who has less physical and mental force.

The experiences of everyday life prove this. The aim of all parents, therefore, should be to teach their children those habits that will result in vigorous health. Children should not be permitted to eat or drink articles that are unhealthful. They should be taught regularity in eating and drinking, in labor, in study, and in sleeping. The body should be cared for and watched over with reference to those rules which experience has proved to be healthful.

DESCRIPTION OF THE ARK OF THE COVE-NANT AND THE TABERNACLE.

Prepared For Sunday School Review.

AFTER a sojourn of 430 years in Egypt, a part of the time in captivity, the Lord by means of Moses and Aaron delivered the children of Israel in a most wonderful manner. In memory of this great event, they were commanded to keep the passover, which ordinance required the eating of unleavened bread for seven days; and it was to be observed as a perpetual memorial throughout all their generations.

The object of the Lord in delivering the people out of bondage into the wilderness, was to bring them to a knowledge of the true God and to induce them to forsake their idolatrous habits and customs before entering the promised land of Canaan.

In order that they might have a place in which to worship the Lord and perform the ordinances that He commanded they were required to build a movable Tabernacle which could be carried from place to place in their journeyings. The Lord sent out a commandment to the people in the following manner:

"Take ye from among you an offering unto the Lord, whosoever is of a willing heart, let him bring it, an offering of the Lord: gold and silver and brass.

' And blue and purple and scarlet and fine linen and goats hair.

' And ram's skin dyed red and badger's skins and shittim wood.

' And oil for the light, and spices for the anointing oil, and for the sweet incense.

''And onyx stones and stones to be set for the ephod and for the breast plate." (*Exodus xxxv 5, 9.*) The people all responded to this call with such willingness, that it was not long before Moses was obliged to send out the proclama-tion that the offerings were to cease as they then had more than sufficient to complete the structure. There the Lord by revelation called Bezaleel to be the general overseer of this great work. The men came and offered their services in the construction of the Temple, while the women made offerings of their personal ornaments such as earrings, bracelets and rings. They also spun the fine linen and the goats hair cloth for the curtains and coverings and beautified them with artistic designs in fine needle work.

This Tabernacle was the tent first erected by Moses in the desert as a visible symbol of the divine presence. It was the place where he went to receive his inspiration as their representative when they came to seek the Lord.

Surrounding the tabernacle was a court 150 feet long and 75 feet broad, formed of curtains, suspended between brass columns with silver trimmings. There were twenty columns on the north and south sides, and ten on the east and west. The entrance was towards the east, that it might receive the first rays of the sun. There were three curtains and three pillars on either side of the gate, which was formed of a costly linen curtain worked with blue, purple and scarlet.

The Tabernacle was forty-five feet wide and fifteen feet high. It was made of boards of acacia wood, as this was the only wood in the country not liable to corruption. They were covered inside and out with gold and fitted together with silver sockets. Three sides of the building were made of these golden covered boards, but the east, or front end, consisted of a curtain which was put aside to form an entrance. Fine linen curtains hung on the inside of the walls as ornaments. Much of the splendor thus lavished was hidden beneath a succession of coverings which constituted the roof and extended down the 'sides nearly if not quite to the ground. The innermost of these coverings displayed the highest art of the day, in the shape of figures of the symbolic cherubim, woven in deep blue, purple and crimson on a white ground of the finest linen. This apparently formed the ceiling and hung down as gorgeous tapestry over the walls. Above this as a protection to it, was laid a second covering of camel hair cloth reaching down the outside almost to the earth. Next came one of ram's skin, dyed red, and, over this the skin of the Dugong, a kind of seal found in the Red Sea.

Josephus says: "And great was the surprise of those that viewed these curtains at a distance, for they seemed not at all to differ from the color of the sky.". The interior of the Tabernacle was divided into two chambers, the eastern forming the Holy Place which was thirty feet by fifteen feet, and the inner or Holy of Holies only fifteen feet square. Like the corresponding space bearing the same name in Egyptian temples, this specially sacred spot was in the west end and was wholly unlighted; for a double curtain of the finest workmanship of many colors and strange forms, veiled it in permanent darkness.

In the north or left hand side of the sanctuary stood the table of Shewbread.

This was three feet long, eighteen inches wide and two feet three inches high, plated with pure gold, and strengthened and ornamented with a gold frame work a hand breadth deep, on which the top rested. Two golden rods passing through four gold rings at the corners supplied the means by which it was carried.

The altar of incense stood in the middle of the sanctuary in front of the veil of the ark. Incense was to be burned on this night and morning for we find in Exodus:

"And Aaron shall burn thereon sweet incense every morning; when he dresseth the lamps he shall burn incense upon it. And when Aaron lighteth the lamps at even he shall burn incense upon it, a perpetual incense before the Lord throughout your generations."

In the south or right side stood the seven branched candlestick, which was of pure gold of beaten work. It stood on one base and spread itself into as many branches as there are planets including the sun. It terminated in seven heads or branches each holding seven lamps. And there were twenty ornaments in all attached to the candlestick.

God commanded the ark to be prepared and placed in the Holy of Holies as a symbol of His having taken possession of it. It was to be three feet nine inches long, two feet three inches wide, and two feet three inches high, made of acacia wood overlaid inside and out with the purest gold. Two rods overlaid with gold ran through the rings which were on each corner of the ark. These rods were never to be removed from the rings lest in taking them out the priests might touch the sacred chest itself. "And when Aaron and his sons have made an end of covering the sanctuary and all the vessels of the sanctuary, the camp is to set forward. After that the sons of Kohath shall come to bear it; but they shall not touch any holy thing lest they die." God commanded Moses to put in the ark the two tables upon which the ten commandments were written, five upon each table.

It required just seven months to complete this Tabernacle and on the first day of the first month of the second year from their exodus it was formally erected in the midst of the camp.

When Moses had completed the work according to all the instructions he had received of the Lord at Mt. Sinai, a cloud covered the tent of the congregation, and the glory of the Lord filled the Tabernacle. There was a cloud upon the Tabernacle by day and fire by night so that they might be continually reminded of its sacred presence. When the cloud was taken up the children of Israel went onward in their journeyings, but if the cloud was not removed they remained in camp.

It would be interesting to further trace the history of the ark, but time forbids. The last mention made of it in the scriptures is during a great feast, when amid solemn ceremonies the ark with all its sacred vessels was placed in the temple of Solomon.

The Lord told Moses to take his brother Aaron and his sons Nadab, Abihu, Eleazar, and Ithamar and ordain them to the office of priests that they might minister unto Him in the holy ordinances of the Tabernacle. Thus we see that on Aaron and his sons was conferred the Aaronic or lesser Priesthood and they were required to officiate in the temporal affairs. The Levitical Priesthood was included in the Aaronic Priesthood, and the sons of Levi were called to settle all the difficulties that arose among the people. The Lord also told Moses to make holy garments after the manner which He should give, and they should be both for glory and for beauty.

The priests were required to minister bare foot and in a cassock of diamond pattern of very fine linen, woven in one piece throughout, which came nearly to the feet, and was secured around the waist by a white linen girdle embroidered with flowers in blue, purple and crimson. This with a round turban, like the cup of a flower completed the costume of the priest. In addition to this dress the high priests wore an upper sleeveless robe of purple, blue woven in one piece elaborately fringed at the neck and ornamented around the skirt, which almost reached the feet, with alternate golden bells and pomegranates of blue, purple, and crimson. Above this came the ephod. A short tunic, with slits for arms like the robe beneath, the back and front being connected by shoulder pieces of broad golden embroidery, in which were inserted two large onyx stones engraved with the names of the twelve tribes, to mark the representative character of the wearer. Over the ephod suspended by golden chains from similar rings, hung a breast plate of the same material as the shoulder piece folded in a square pocket, a span in size each way. On this were twelve precious stones set in gold in four rows. The first row was composed of a sardius, a topas, and a carbuncle. The second row was an emerald, a sapphire and a diamond. The third row consisted of a ligure, an agate, and an amethyst, and the fourth row a beryl, an onyx and a jasper. Also up on the front of the mitre or turban was a plate of pure gold upon which was engraved like the engravings of a signet, Holiness to The Lord.

The priests were only allowed to go into the sanctuary and to perform the ordinances there, but the High Priests were to officiate in the Holy of Holies, which they entered but once a year owing to the sacredness of the spot.

Grace Freeze.

Our Little Folks.

FOR THE LETTER BOX.

DEAR LETTER BOX.—My father is on a mission. He was real sick and mamma felt very bad about him. One Tuesday morning she went to the Temple to have my little brother Charley blest, because he suffered so much with the ear-ache. After they came home, mother said, "Oh! if I could only know how your father is!" Charley was surprised to hear that, and said, "Why! of course he is well now, mamma!" "How do you know?" mother asked. Charley said, "Why! didn't you hear that man in the Temple pray for the missionaries this morning? Didn't he mean papa with the rest? Of course he did! Papa is all right!" The next day, we got a letter from papa which said he was real well. And Charley's ears haven't ached since, and it is more than three weeks.

Pauline Preid, 10 years old.

SALT LAKE CITY UTAH.

DEAR LETTER BOX.—We have one of the kindest and best dogs any of our folks have ever known. Her name is Goodey, and it is true for her.

When any of us are sick, or if the children cry about anything, she whines about, and acts as if she would be so glad to help us.

She is a shepherd dog, and knows everyone of our cows and calves and sheep and lambs from all the others around. In the evening, she will bring all of ours home, and drive them into the yard, but she will not let one go in that is not ours.

Goodey seems to know Sunday, and to like it as well as the rest of us. When father lets the bars down, or I do, about half past seven Sunday morning, she drives all the stock out of the yard, but she keeps watch and does not let any of them stray off, as on other days. And when father brings out the horses, or lets me, to take us to Sunday School, at about half past nine, Goodey hurries up and drives all the stock in again, so we can put up the bars, and then she is ready to lie on the doorstep and keep watch of things until we get home again. Then she jumps about, and is so glad, it does us all good to see her.

Father speaks as lovingly to her as if she were a child; mother pats her kindly; we boys hug her, and our baby sister lets Goodey kiss her hands and face, and laughs about it.

Father says Goodey is worth more to him in some ways than two or three men could be; and she costs nothing but for her food, which is not much.

Goodey is black with brown spots about her eyes. Her coat is a little shaggy, and she has a short tail.

I think everyone should be good to dogs. *Frank H. Aged 11 years.*

LITTLE RANCH, UTAH.

DEAR LITTLE CHILDREN.—We had a birthday party on the 25th of March. We danced, and had a good time, only that little Joseph Watkins was taken sick and could not dance. That night, after I went home, I was saying my prayer, and I prayed for Joseph, that he might not be sick long. And he got well and was at school the next day. I know that our kind Heavenly Father hears the prayers of His children who love Him.

Mary Lovland. Aged 12 years.

PARIS, IDAHO, April, 1897.

EDITOR OF THE JUVENILE:—In reading your paper I find some nice stories written by small children, so I will try and relate a story of Esquimaux and how they live.

The Esquimaux are considerably higher in the scale of civilization than the Indians. Living in a clime where existence is a constant struggle, they have developed higher qualities than their red brothers. Their huts are simple, yet, they contain many comforts. The huts are built of cakes of ice, which, when frozen solidly together and covered with snow, are quite warm. These contain rude chairs, tables, and other articles of furniture. No stoves are used, but in their place are great lamps in which is burned the oil and blubber from whales and walruses. These lamps give both light and heat, but send forth a bad smell, and soon cover everything in the hut with a coat of grimy soot.

Women and men dress much alike and, owing to severe cold, are obliged to wear garments of fur which they get from the seal, the silver fox, the polar bear, and other animals with valuable fur. Their food is mostly meat; the fat of the animal being deemed a great luxury. In fact, a tallow candle is as great a treat to the Esquimaux as is a bon bon to an American girl, while a brimming cup of oil is sweeter to the Esquimaux boy than is champagne to his American brother. Their home life is pleasant and affectionate. The women are treated with considerable respect though they cheerfully bear their part of the household burden. Their time is spent in hunting such game as the polar bear, the walrus, with now and then a chase after a whale which wanders into their waters. They are a quiet inoffensive people, with many good traits. You will remember hearing of their village at the World's Fair where,

perhaps, no other strange people attracted more attention than they did.

Alfred Michel, 15 years of age.

RANDOLPH, RICH Co.
April 4th, 1897.

I AM but a little girl. But I like the little letters that come in the JUVENILE. I have a little brother named for Apostle Lyman. I think he is cute. He can walk. We have a dog named Cap, and baby plays with him on the door step.

I love to go to Sunday School. The class I belong to has three loving teachers. Their names are Sister Fackrel, Sister Grant and Sister Speucer. They teach us a great many good things.

It would have been so nice if we could all have seen President Woodruff, and been at the celebration on his birthday. Our schools were closed here, and we went to the meeting-house, and had a good time.

I send my love to all the little letter writers.

Florabell Gray. Age 9 years.

HUNTSVILLE, WEBER Co., UTAH.
February 12th, 1897.

EDITOR JUVENILE INSTRUCTOR:—Having seen a number of sketches in the JUVENILE INSTRUCTOR I thought I would write a short sketch of my life.

I was born at Huntsville, Weber County, Utah, December 23rd, 1881, which was the date that the Prophet Joseph Smith was born. I was baptized the day I became eight years of age. That day I will never forget, as it was a special fast day for all the Saints of God. Soon after I was baptized I was taken very ill with scarlet fever. I was very low and lost my speech for a long time. My parents sent for the Elders and through the anointing of oil and the prayer of faith I was healed. I was ordained a Deacon January 8th, 1894, at Huntsville, in which quorum I am still laboring. My father is on a mission to Denmark. He started on the 25th of January, 1896. A short time after he left I hired out to work to help support him on his mission and to help the family. I have earned my own clothes and sent my father $40.00 to help him, so he could buy tracts and do a good work. My desire is to live so I can inherit a place in the Kingdom of our Lord.

Henry J. J. Nielson.

LIBERTY, UTAH,
March. 29th, 1897.

DEAR LETTER BOX.—Our baby is two years and twenty-four days old. He has eighteen teeth. His eyes are dark-brown. His hair is light and curly. His name is Parley. We live in Ogden valley. It is very stormy. The snow is three feet and a half deep here. It has been five feet deep.

Sarah Judkins.

DEAR LETTER BOX:—Camels are very useful animals. Men use them to cross deserts, because horses cannot travel over such large, sandy plains, the horse does not have large feet, and camels have.

When men are on deserts and a wind storm is coming up, the camel will lie down and the men will too. The sand will not then get in their eyes. The camel has a large hump on his back. When the men are going to start out on their journey, they feel of the humps to see if they are hard. If there is not quite enough fat in them, the men will wait a while and feed them well. He has hard skin on his knees and under the neck. All camels are not the same. Some have two humps. The camel is the best animal for the deserts. He will drink all he wants, then he will feel the sacks that are in his stomach.

When he is on the desert and is thirsty, he will drink one of the sacks of water. The water in the sacks will last him till he gets across the deserts. When the camel is over with his journey, the hump has gone down quite a lot. The camel can smell water far off. He can carry very heavy things.

He is a very tall animal, and has long legs.

There are little spots of grass on the deserts. There are not any trees. It is very hot. It does not rain on the deserts. The sand is very deep.

The camel is very kind to his master. The men speak and sing praises of their camels because they are so kind to them. Here is a verse that they sometimes say:

"Camel thou art good and mild,
Might be guided by a child;
And these desert wastes must be
Untracked regions but for thee."

Leonard K. Jones. Age 7 years.
BLUFF, SAN JUAN CO., UTAH.

TOLD OF SIR ANDREW CLARK.

SIR ANDREW CLARK was so ardent in his crusade against overeating and over-drinking, and so firm in his belief that in a large majority of cases diet will do far more than drugs, that he was a little too much inclined to take it for granted that his patients were self-indulgent to the ruin of their health. Among the many anecdotes of which his views gave rise the following is one of the most amusing:

A patient came to consult him, and was at once overwhelmed with directions on the subject of the life he should lead and the diet to which he should adhere. "Now, remember, only one glass of wine at each meal," the physician concluded, "and just one cigar after dinner won't hurt you. Good morning. Be sure you keep strictly to the one cigar."

"One cigar!" said the patient. "But——"

"My dear sir," broke in Sir Andrew somewhat testily, "I must insist. If I am to treat you, you must follow my directions. I know quite well you will find it hard, but it is absolutely necessary for your health."

The patient heaved a deep sigh. "All right, Sir Andrew; since you insist I will do my best. Good mcrning."

He went his way, but his healtth did not improve, and at the end of a few weeks he returned to the physician's consulting room.

"No better?" said the Doctor, surprised. "But have you followed all my directions?"

"Absolutely," replied the visitor. "I must admit that the cigar was rather hard work at first, and in fact made me feel very ill; but I soon got used to it, and now I rather like it."

"Good heavens!" said Sir Andrew on whom the truth dawned, "do you mean to tell me—"

"Yes, I had never smoked before."

If this world of ours is ever to be made better than it is, it is to be made better by believing in it and taking its inherent goodness for granted. By making men despise, doubt, question, disbelieve themselves, you will never induce them to improve themselves.

HONEST TIMES.

When it Was an Insult to Ask for a Receipt for Money.

AT one time in the Highlands of Scotland to ask for a receipt or promissory note was considered an insult, and such a thing as a breach of contract was rarely heard of, so strictly did the people regard their honor. The Presbyterian Witness tells a story of a farmer who had been to the Lowlands and had there acquired worldly wisdom.

After returning to his native place he needed some money, and requested a loan from a gentleman in the neighborhood. The latter, Mr. Stewart, complied and counted out the gold, when the farmer immediately wrote a receipt.

"And what is this, man?" cried Mr. Stewart, on receiving the slip of paper.

"That is a receipt, sir, binding me to give ye back your gold at the right time," replied Donald.

"Binding ye, indeed! Well, my man, if ye canna trust yoursel, I'm sure I'll na trust ye! Such as ye canna hae my gold;" and gathering it up he returned it to his desk and locked it up.

"But, sir, I might die," replied the needy Scot, unwilling to surrender his hope of the loan; "and perhaps my sons might refuse it ye, but the bit of paper would compel them."

"Compel them to sustain their dead father's honor!" cried the enraged Celt. "They'll need compelling to do right, if this is the road ye're leading them. Ye can gang elsewhere for money, I tell ye; but ye'll find nane about here that'll put more faith in a bit of paper than a neighbor's word of honor and his love of right."

THE man who wastes time wastes money.

A ——— **School Desks** Just
Carload **School Desks** Received.

No waiting for goods. Lowest Prices. Send your orders in before the sizes
you want are gone.
A full line of Maps, Charts. Globes, Blackboards, always on hand.

WRITE FOR CATALOGUE AND PRICES.

W. S. PIERCE,

TELEPHONE NO. 577.

501, 505, 507 Constitution Building, - **SALT LAKE CITY, UTAH.**

ELIAS MORRIS & SONS CO.,

SALT LAKE CITY.

Benjamin Franklin once said: "I only need visit the graveyard of a community to know the character of the people."

In doing your part toward the preservation of the people's character in this direction, you will find it much to your advantage to deal with the largest firm in this region of the country. We will give you the lowest figures for the best class of workmanship. Write for prices and designs.

ELIAS MORRIS & SONS CO.,

21 to 30 W. South Temple Street.

OPPOSITE ENTRANCE TO TEMPLE BLOCK.

GRANITE AND MARBLE MONUMENTS AND HEADSTONES

Lightning Source UK Ltd.
Milton Keynes UK
UKHW010430091118
332016UK00007B/129/P